Ancien

for

Reality Creators

50 pages that could change your life

Easy & Healing Steps to Redefining Success & Creating a Life of Well-Being, Happiness, & Wonder, Or an Enlightening & Transformative Discovery of Wisdom for Creating a Life of Authentic Awakening, Emotional Freedom & Practical Spirituality.

By Tony Samara

TONYSAMARA

Copyright

problems without the advice of a physician, either directly or indirectly. The intent of the author is only to offer information of a general nature to help you in your quest for emotional and spiritual well-being. In the event you use any of the information in this book for yourself, which is your constitutional right, the author and the publisher assume no responsibility for your actions.

To order additional copies of Tony Samara's book and eBooks, contact:

Amazon USA:
http://astore.amazon.com/tonysamahumaa-20
Amazon UK: http://astore.amazon.co.uk/tonsam-21

Published by

Tony Samara Books
http://www.tonysamarabooks.com
info@tonysamara.org

Table of Contents

Foreword

"As soon as we recognize that the mind and the ego do not offer satisfactory answers on our quest for Happiness, for Love, for Joy, for Peace and for Spirituality, and that any fight, any research and any waiting for something separate and outside of ourselves is a waste of time, then we can experience freedom. To let go of this belief is really magical.
One calms down quite naturally and in this peace One can be in touch with Totality.

Like the Phoenix rising out of the ashes, a new attitude emerges for life. A comprehension is formed in our hearts. We can reorient our beliefs and create a foundation for freedom and transformation. This place of understanding from which we feel comfortable in all circumstances comes from inner peace rather than from waiting or researching anything. Then each step we take on our path naturally becomes an expression of Freedom, Joy and Love."

~ Sat Tony Samara

Introduction

It is wonderful that spiritual practice can be part of your life wherever you are and need not be limited by external situations or formal settings. To assist people in the practice of their personal spirituality, **Sat Tony Samara** has completed writing the following discourses as an inspiration for everyone during life's multitude of many and varied situations.

Together we can create a beautiful world.

Thank you!

The CMF Team

Chapter 1 – Divine Ecstasy

"Within each of us is a light, awake, encoded in the fibers of our existence. Divine ecstasy is the totality of this marvelous creation experienced in the hearts of humanity"
~ Sat Tony Samara

It is interesting that most people reach a point in their lives where they accept the feeling of being alive but not quite to the extent that they wish this aliveness to be. Divine ecstasy is the ecstasy one feels that is beyond the joy and happiness that comes from the mundane aspects of life and this status quo feeling.

Divine ecstasy is found naturally within each one of us and it is the wonderful bridge that connects us to all humanity and gives us the feeling of being one with all of creation, that we are experiencing in our lives right now.

Unfortunately, the ego which searches for the mundane happiness through the senses and the satisfaction of the material aspects of our existence is like a thin patch of cloud that prevents the true light of our hearts from being seen.

It is often so cloudy for most of us with all the activities of daily life that our inner selves forget that there is a light beyond this patch of cloud. What does it take for this cloud to disperse so that we can again see the beautiful light of the sun that is shining naturally around all humanity?

The ego is like a divider dividing what can be experienced into two aspects. It creates the impression that we are separate aspects of creation - that you are one, I am another and so forth. When the ego vanishes, that is, when the ego again connects to the aspect of ourselves that is deeper than the mundane, the aspect of ourselves that is beyond the senses and detached from materialism, then we will realize our own inner consciousness that connects us to the evolution of human consciousness.

I have been asked where does this evolution lead us? This can be answered in two very simple words. SELFLESS LOVE.

When we go beyond judging others and ourselves through the aspect that judges, which is the ego, then we don't condemn ourselves to the superficial but rather give birth to our depth which is embodied through the aspect of love that we are all born with.

What can we do in a practical sense so that the ego and our true self can dwell as intimate friends in the same body?

I believe that one great step is to detach ourselves from the mundane aspects that grab our attention in daily life and rather than feed the ego with food that doesn't nourish it, why not perform kind acts that help us to see what love means in action.

This love in action can be measured in many ways. It is not simply being nice or saying nice things to people but rather going deeply into the energy that divides us from the sense of love. This energy can also be measured in many ways. In our modern world it is surely measured to a great extent in the form of monetary wealth.

There is nothing wrong with monetary wealth when we see that it is a form of energy for us to share and in this understanding the more wealth the better. This is the new paradigm for the era that we are entering. Rather than a poverty mentality of there not being enough or having to struggle in an impoverished world, why not realise that the abundance, i.e. the wealth, exists.

Many of us forget that money is a form of energy that is, in today's world, often expressed in a selfish way. Whatever we have in a monetary sense we like to hold onto, in the hope that it will fulfill happiness, by fulfilling mundane and material aspects that the ego believes will nourish ourselves with happiness and love. This belief system needs to change to an expression of what we all deeply want: LOVE.

I believe that the best way for love to increase is by giving rather than holding on. In this light we know that to receive we need to give. As we learn this in action and through practical means by truly giving, then we open ourselves to receive unlimited abundance. As we release our limited programmes and belief systems of impoverishment we allow the new experience of giving to become part of our enlightened belief system.

Following this philosophy, I encourage you all to consider contributing unconditionally 10% of your savings if any and 10% of your monthly earnings to a humanitarian, ecological or spiritual cause of your choice in the knowledge that this action of love will again awaken the true self into realising itself in the oneness of life.

When we as individuals realise this then surely we change the world.

Chapter 2 – Changing the Old Ways

*"When we can unite the in breath with the out breath,
we honour our origins and create
beautiful harmony."*
~ *Sat Tony Samara*

As we move inwardly during the winter months, this inward movement is best approached without our personal limitations. Better that it be viewed as a gateway to embracing more freedom beyond set patterns, thoughts and old ways of doing things.

These old ways need to change for us to actually see that change is possible and I feel that the below questions provide a wonderful opportunity to meditate upon and thereby open ourselves more to the endless possibilities of life.

Is it good to feel enjoyment?

It is very good to feel happy and it is very good to feel enjoyment. Yet it is as, or even more, important to know the depth of what makes those aspects of ourselves become alive and real so that those feelings of happiness and enjoyment have a more permanent duration to them rather than simply being a temporary satisfaction of external desires leading to good feelings. If the I (ego) is involved in the feelings it will be on a constant and endless search to satisfy what makes it happy and that is the same circle as the mind seeking its salvation in the problems of unhappiness and not realising its deeper essence.

Is it good to look in other directions?

All directions come back to who you are and what you do. I am sure you understand that it is not the directions that bring you back to yourself (your essence) but rather the enlightened teacher that helps you to see that some curves and twists even though seemingly on the surface are taking you straight to a place of what seems to be the solution to your problems, are in actual fact just that... curves and twists. Hence, as the reminder of your inner guide, I must make you aware that you are curving and twisting rather than going directly to the space that will help you see clearly. Being clear means to be less serious. Remember the light. There is no need to weigh yourself down with the excess baggage of the games that the mind likes to play, anticipating that happiness and enjoyment are found in the shadows of the mind, rather than in the light of your essence.

Can I trust you?

Can you trust yourself? Many of us who have enquired deeply into ourselves have realised through the layers of what makes us human - our mind, our emotions, our body, our limitations - that really it is difficult to trust such human aspects in their incompleteness as they are always seeking salvation by fulfilling needs rather than moving beyond those needs and opening up to giving more. If the reference point is to find freedom and happiness then reflect on what is more truly a picture of such a reference by loving and giving rather than being distrustful and giving power to fears and limitations of the mind, body and emotions.

Surely the question of trust comes from a fearful, dualistic mind thinking that there is a separation between you and I. Trusting is not about fear of others or yourself, shepherds or sheep, good or bad, right or wrong, it is much deeper. It is about trusting. The more we trust the more we are able to love as love embodies trust. If we approach love from a trusting space, then if this love is all-embracing and real, how can it not be worth your trust? On a practical level, my work with everyone, including you, goes beyond such mundane separations such as distrust.

Whether you are aware of love or not makes no difference as love goes beyond the normal senses and into the divine spaces of unknowingness. Soon you will know this space as you trust it more. Be aware that the clever mind creates a veil that clouds our thinking and perceptions - twisting and curving and moving us away from giving and loving and creating the perception of lacks and judgments that create needs and desires.

Trust what you know and do what is natural - give directly from the heart.

Chapter 3 – Joyous Expansion

"The miracle of life and enjoying all its abundance leads humanity to a creative reflection that deepens our experience of this wondrous miracle. This miracle is so often forgotten because of the thoughts and feelings that well up and colour the simplicity of each moment and its unique gifts. To savour these gifts it is essential to remember that our desires for more, or something different, or something special, is often camouflaging the very essence of what feeds our heart, what enriches our experience, what deepens our feelings and what centers our thinking back to a sense of gratitude and love. Live simply and appreciate this simplicity by appreciating what is, what you have and who you are, thus allowing this moment to be savoured in its completeness.
Let's live life rather than chase the idea of life!"
~ Sat Tony Samara

How to touch and expand the joy that is our essence but that is often veiled by the mundane and its demands on our time?

Joy is not static, or a place, or even a goal but rather, like art and music, multi-faceted, uncontainable and expansive.

The way to experience joy is unique to each individual, yet the core of joy is a shared experience that makes us human and part of an alive participating adventure.

Simply put, joy is only understood through the expansion of consciousness. This is when we glimpse what it means to be expansive.
Most of us, due to a thousand and one reasons, focus on the lacks, limitations and problems. These lacks, limitations and problems are so real that they demand all of our attention and from this space we struggle to find the real joy of each moment.

Many feel that by resolving what seems to be a block or hindrance for their expansion then expansion will happen miraculously. I see it differently.

What we want is what we need to be.

An oak tree starts as an acorn but it has no doubt that it will fulfill its destiny as a tree. Most of us don't even believe that possibilities and potential are real as our experience sabotages our expansion and holds us in the mud of daily living.

The sky, the light, the beautiful stars seem to come from a different world and seem totally out of reach.

This leads to depression as we no longer believe in our destiny or even see the light.

One of the most important steps to reawaken who we really are is to be of service to humanity. By being of service to humanity rather than to our perceived needs, we remember in our actions the true meaning of love.

Love is expansive. As we expand with this service so does our focus expand, freeing our attachment to the mud, so that we are harmoniously in touch with the Universe.

It is not a difficult journey if put into action, but it does seem impossible when one uses the present contracting situation as a limitation to what is possible, and hence why many of us are not able to expand.

I ask you strongly during these intense times not to focus on yourselves or your needs, or the problems, or the lack of joy, or what could be better. No matter how present they seem, please focus on what it means to serve others and the divine aspect of what is their essence.

As you begin to see the light in every being there is no doubt in my mind that the light within will help the acorn that is in each of us to reach up and open to this new and beautiful expansive experience and hence open up to the joy of life.

This is what is asked of us during this special time. It is up to each of you to put this into practice rather than to just meditate upon the beauty of my words. The world needs more trees.

Chapter 4 – Societal Excesses

"When confronted with the excesses of societal,
family and other personal dynamics be patient,
compassionate and diligent"
~ Sat Tony Samara

In today's world of materialism and consumerism we often forget the energy behind the products that we buy in the places where we shop. Advertising, social pressures and the sense of separation that industrial mass-production creates, encourages people to forget that the most important part of the gift, or an object, is its feeling and sense of beauty. Cheapness, and the negative energy that is associated with the pain and suffering that is part of the sweatshops and unethical mass-producing factories cycle, often creates the sense of materialism where true value is distorted. I encourage you to purchase products from ethical companies that have a genuine interest in its workers and the people buying the products and in creating a new paradigm whereby what is being created is not a cheap throw-away product but rather something that can be deeply appreciated and carry with it the beauty of giving.

Chapter 5 – Service to Humanity

*Often the simple things in life are a gateway to
well-being and happiness. Live simply.
Be conscious of your actions and
support conscious actions."
~ Sat Tony Samara*

Service to humanity is such an amazing gift in this
seemingly more self-centered world of ours today. We
can learn that the world does not centre around
ourselves, our needs, our beliefs, or even our
thoughts or words but rather centers around love,
centers around our expansion beyond ego and into a
space where spiritual growth, compassion,
cooperation and focused giving to others, to the
world, to mother earth, to the universal goodness is
the magical heart of existence. The creative meaning
of existence helps us to nourish our needs, beliefs and
thoughts from a space that transcends limitations,
dependencies and expectations in a practical as well
as in a philosophical sense.

In a practical sense we need to watch the mind and
the ego to avoid the games that are so often created
to justify our actions. If working in a garden, and our
efforts and time spent in the garden are simply to
satisfy our selfish needs, then we bypass so much and

we miss the beauty of sharing our efforts with all that is present and alive. If we plant trees as a gift to humanity then those trees flourish. If we plant them simply to satisfy needs then we don't have a forest rather we have an extension of, or a picture of, our needs in the garden lacking in the aliveness and magic that is so natural to this world.

In the same sense, if any other action or practical work that we undertake is simply to satisfy our needs and we surely forget the beauty of the world and to be an integral part of this beauty, then our work becomes self-centered and its goal becomes to satisfy our beliefs, needs, egos and thoughts. Being and trusting that your real and selfless actions are an expression of beauty, then those beliefs, needs, thoughts and egotistical aspects become superfluous and we enter an aliveness and magic that is our birthright.

This is what makes people great and gives meaning to our personal life as well as hope for humanity.

Chapter 6 – Deep Spiritual Work

"By being of selfless service to others
you touch the heart of humanity."
~ Sat Tony Samara

Deep spiritual work means not following desires or what the mind is seemingly telling you is the truth but rather honouring the depth of who you are.

You are, quite simply, an amazing being and this can be experienced directly through the mind, body and feelings when they are totally clear and in touch with your heart. Most people use the mind only for thinking and, without the connection to the deeper aspects of themselves, think they know everything without knowing anything. Not that this experience is unwarranted, as perhaps they need this experience to find out what their truth is by consciously eliminating all the circles that take them away from their being and essence.

It is always best to trust not what feels nice or what seems right but rather what is. Most of the time our beliefs about what constitutes our essence come from a space of lack rather than from a space of appreciation for the fullness of our being. We seek to fulfill that space of lack with external things that we think will complete it. Of course this does not bring us completeness. Most people act and think in this contradictory way - more money, more comfort, more things, more, more, more means happiness and unfortunately most people take too long to experience the disappointment that this is not true.

In the end I can tell you what to do but the circling only stops when what creates the momentum to do the circling disappears. I am not saying that basic comforts are unimportant but they will not fulfill your inner joy. It is the embracing and the experiencing of your inner joy that will enable you to stop the circling.

At this point of human evolution it is the optimum moment to transcend these circles by utilising some simple wisdoms.

One good thing to do is to write down in a journal the specifics of what makes you feel the way you do about whatever your situation is and find a positive attribute that can make you feel better about this situation.

This simple yet profound exercise will help you to unload conditioned responses and become less reactive to addictive behaviours, stresses and other strains that the mind likes to occupy itself with.

Secondly, what is important is to generate energy, clarity and peace as a response to your experience of life. This is done by simply focusing your thoughts or feelings away from the circling behaviours and onto the breath of life. By focusing on the breath of life you help to balance what creates distractions within you and you are able to move to a new level of awareness.

This breath helps you to integrate your experiences rather than continuing the circles that create your sense of separation. This breath can make you feel so much more centered giving you a natural sense of joy and integration with the experiences that you are facing, no matter what they are. This joy and integration means you are not pulled in different directions but simply experience the moment as it is. This more awakened way of experiencing helps you to function from a space where the mind seems to transcend the mundane and is then able to stop flitting from one thing to another.

With the regular practice of this way of breathing your mind becomes ever more quiet, and more able to focus on the breath, helping to elevate the physical body to a sense of pureness, which then naturally encompasses the mind and emotions.

This meditation exercise can be practiced anywhere.

To begin the exercise of breathing the breath of life it is necessary to remember to breathe through your nose. Then allow the breath to be focused on the body by bringing your attention to a mystical point that is approximately three finger widths below the navel. When you breathe into this point you are able to expand the diaphragm, relaxing into a deep breath, so that the lungs fill with breath from the bottom to the top. As you exhale the breath, the belly and diaphragm totally relax allowing for a full and complete exhalation.

What you are doing is taking a pure, deep and total breath with no emotion and with no thought. It is simply a breath that is deeply connected to this point in your body, which then allows you in every moment and with every breath to exquisitely feel the depth of the breath and of your being. It feels almost like waves on the beach coming and going with no connection to anything but the wonderful movement of itself.

By doing this you will be able to dip into a well of rejuvenation and tranquility where everything is seen from a clearer perspective allowing you to awaken to a feeling of completeness and to experience a sense of oneness and connectedness with the fascinating play of life.

This guidance may not make the circling aspects of yourself easily disappear but rather help you to embrace them in the best possible way. Embracing the depth of who you are brings a new vitality and lightness into your amazing being.

Chapter 7 – The Light of Conscious Awareness

*"Get to know your thoughts and the inner
processes of your mind and emotions. Delete the
negatives that limit your self. Create a healthier
reality, a healthier inner space, and a healthier
belief system for your life, through your
wonderful actions. Your essence will emerge from
this nurturing and you will feel renewed and
ready to truly celebrate a new cycle of life
- the rebirth of the light."
~ Sat Tony Samara*

**Discover that your ideas are constantly being
given shape and material form on this earthly
level.**

Every thought, every aspect of your creative mind and
imagination results in an adventure of possibilities.
Possibilities that may excite the heart and open you
up to a world where the boundaries of normal
limitations fade into insignificance as you expand
beyond what the ego-mind says and listen to your
innate wisdom.

A wisdom which belongs to no-one as it is the shared
oneness open to be explored by everyone deeply
during these next coming months. A wisdom

contained beyond the limiting formulas or dogmas of the past. Behold this new gift being birthed!

More intensely than ever, the inner work leads us now to light, to unity, from a troubled mind to an open heart and, hence, to the profoundness of love.

This journey leads us to the realisation of who we are. What an opportunity to have a guide on this spiritual journey to help all successfully traverse the spiritual path.

I welcome you into the possibility of self-enquiry and discovery of your deepest truth.

I welcome you to an opportunity to recognise that whatever is going on is a mirror, a clear reflection, telling you more about yourself even though this may not seem so in the turbulent moments.

That whoever you think you are is not your reality. It is not your essence. Your essence is beyond the activity of thought or belief systems and when this stops even for an instant you open a gateway to another world that will give you strength and courage to reveal the truth that we all share and that is beyond such dualism.

When the theatre of the mundane aspects of the ego is transcended, when our attention is directed in an honest way into truthful knowing, the heart is freed from the chains that seem so heavy. This gives us an opportunity to discover that whatever concept or emotion is honestly or directly examined, miraculously loses its grip, freeing us to experience happiness.

The light of conscious awareness that is produced from this moment of happiness penetrates the ego and its games, making it impossible for suffering to continue its position of authority and hold on our lives.

ABOUT THE AUTHOR

Tony Samara

Founder of the
Conscious Meditation Foundation
and the Samara School of Meditation

Tony Samara, author of 'Shaman's Wisdom,' 'The Simplicity of Love Meditation,' 'Different Yet the Same,' 'Karma, Mantra and Beyond' and 'Discover Your Inner Buddha' was born in England, grew up in Egypt, England, and also in Norway where he discovered the "Zen Buddhist philosophy".

This discovery eventually led him to the Mount Baldy Zen Center in California, USA, where he learned the spiritual teachings of Kyozan Joshu Sasaki. He had curiosity to explore further the essence of spirituality and thus went to live and learn with shamanic communities around the globe. By going on pilgrimage to various sacred sites in India, Tony was able to dwell deeply upon the ancient Vedic and Jain philosophies and work profoundly with the essence of these teachings. He says:

"My first spiritual teacher, at the age of 12, was the question "Who Am I?" Over a few years, as I immersed myself deeper into the question, in many different countries and through various spiritual traditions, in a universalist open-minded way, gradual and powerful experiences opened me up more and more until at the age of 27 I experienced a dramatic moment of enlightenment.

Today, inspired deeply by the words of Shrimad Rajchandra and Mahavira and the poetry of Satguru Kabir, I share with you the totally natural state of joy and wisdom experienced as the heart opens to the truth."

"As real self I never knew,
So suffered I eternal pain,
I bow to Him my master true,
Who preached and broke eternal chain."
~ Shrimad Rajchandra, Atmasiddhi - 1.1

*"There within Him creation goes forward,
which is beyond all philosophy;
for philosophy cannot attain to Him:
There is an endless world, O my Brother!
and there is the Nameless Being,
of whom nought can be said."*
~ *Satguru Kabir*

Now people from all over the world visit Tony Samara to take spiritual guidance and experience being in his presence.

Tony Samara believes that "the vast majority of people go through life without directly experiencing the depths of their true self, or understanding their connection to life, or their relationship to others and to the world at large. We are often taught to only relate to the world through our senses. We think, we reason, we feel - but we do not know from our hearts what it means to be connected to what is beyond the senses."

He recognizes that direct experiences have the potential to radically transform an individual and his or her life, as well as promote a profound and effortless letting go of past emotional, mental and physical pain and suffering.

His main countries of activity are in Europe, yet with the assistance of the Internet he is attracting a Global audience through frequent online interviews and live satsangs. His function is as a Spiritual Master who encourages all to lead their lives actively in a noble way in order to realize the evolution of human consciousness.

Verbal dialogue is not the essence of his teachings, but he explains in a direct and simple way that everyone can understand how each individual can practically integrate greater acceptance, peace and joy into their daily lives.

Tony Samara teaches with humour, humility and with infinite patience, empowering the individual with courage, trust and inner strength to continue on this journey back into wholeness, a path that leads towards real freedom.

Join **Tony Samara in person at the many meditation programmes** available.

We invite you to visit the programme page of http://www.TonySamara.com to find the nearest **programme** where you can experience the energy transmission and wisdoms, which often are beyond description in words.

There are also many easy possibilities to work with Tony Samara from the comfort of your own home by joining the **online satsangs** http://www.tonysamara.co.uk/blog/satsangs/

To subscribe to the mailing list please write to us at info@tonysamara.org and we will gladly update you with all the latest news and inspirational quotes!

In Honour of Mahavira

*"O Self! Practice Truth, and nothing but Truth.
Enlightened by the light of Truth,
the wise transcend death.
Truth alone is the essence in the world."
~ Mahavira*

If you want to cultivate a habit,
do it without any reservation,
til it is firmly established.
Until it is so confirmed,
until it becomes a part of your character,
Let there be no exception,
no relaxation of effort."
~ Mahavira

Conscious Meditation has a direct energetic connection to **Mahavira** and the Jain lineage due to its emphasis on the triple gems of Jainism — conscious vision or view, conscious knowledge and conscious conduct — which constitute the path to consciousness and liberation. These three gems are essential for the soul to transcend spiritually.

Mahavira (599 BCE–527 BCE) was the twenty-fourth and last Supreme Master (Tirthankara). (A Supreme Master dwells exclusively within the realm of their Soul, and is entirely free of inner attachments and personal desires. As a result of this they possess unlimited spiritual powers, that are readily available to them and which they use exclusively for the spiritual elevation of living beings.)

Although Mahavira is widely regarded as the founder of Jainism, he is more properly regarded as a reformer of Jainism.

Mahavira was born into a royal family in what is now India. At the age of 30 he left his home in pursuit of spiritual awakening (Diksha). For the next twelve and a half years he practiced intense meditation, after which he achieved enlightenment. He traveled all over India for the next thirty years to teach his philosophy, which is based on the five principals found in Appendix 5.

Mahavira attained supreme consciousness (nirvana) at the age of 72.

Mahavira taught that pursuit of pleasure is an endless game, so we should train our minds to curb individual addictions and attachments. That way one achieves equanimity of mind, mental poise and spiritual balance. So, the individual or society should exercise self-restraint to achieve social peace, security and an enlightened society.

Mahavira said, "We should forgive our own soul first. To forgive others is a practical application of this supreme forgiveness. It is the path of spiritual purification."

Mahavira also said, "Anger begets more anger and forgiveness and love beget more forgiveness and love. Forgiveness benefits both the forgiver and the forgiven."

In Honour of Shrimad Rajchandra

Conscious Meditation has a direct energetic connection to **Shrimad Rajchandra's** lineage due to its core values of *Ahimsa* (peacefulness) and loving kindness. These being essentially the same as those propagated by **Shrimad Rajchandra**.

Shri Raichandbhai Ravjibhai Mehta (later known as **Shrimad Rajchandra**) was born in Vavania, Gujarat, India.

His father, Ravjibhai, was of Vaishnav (a branch of Hinduism) background, and his wife Devbai, followed a Jain lifestyle. Shrimad's mother was a model of humility and service and despite being financially poor, Devbai continued to serve monks, saints and all visitors to her home with generosity and kindness.

When Shrimad was seven years of age, an elder and fond friend, Amichandbhai, died of a snakebite. As he pondered deeply the question of life and death, wondering why someone would burn a man when he died, suddenly he felt as though a veil had been removed and he experienced 'Jati Smarana Gnan,' meaning he remembered the knowledge of his previous births! A small temple stands today at this location.

Even at this early age he showed great determination and completed seven standards of curriculum in only two years. He started his poet's career at the age of eight, writing about a thousand stanzas in the first year and composed the classics 'Ramayana' and 'Mahabharat' in verse when he was only nine.

He was only 16 when he composed a book explaining simply and lucidly the essence of Jain teachings. He also composed the Mokshamala (Rosary of Moksha) of 108 lessons, which even today provides wonderful insights into a true spiritual life, Jain teachings and the meaning of certain practices. Even today it provides inspiration to thousands.

Shrimad Rajchandra, taught the Truth to many people, one of whom was Mahatma Gandhi. Mahatma Gandhi met Shrimad when the sage was 25 years old and was captivated by his depth on spiritual and religious matters and was deeply influenced by him more so even than Tolstoy and Ruskin. He says:

"This man has won my heart in spiritual matters and no one else has ever made on me the same impression."
– Mahatma Gandhi, Modern Review, June 1930

At the age of 23, Shrimad attained Self-Realisation. He spent months of seclusion in jungles and mountains, absorbed in the ecstasy of the Self.

His compassion for the world overflowed, when he was 28 years old, in the form of the 'Atma Siddhi Shastra,' a masterpiece in philosophical literature. Composed of 142 stanzas it explains the Jain path to liberation (Moksha). It was written in only 90 minutes, one night.

In 1901, at the age of 33, this Enlightened Soul left His mortal body, in a state of complete awareness.

Shrimad often spoke about the various religions being prisons in which men are prisoners and that whoever wants liberation should jump out of them. That we are guided by the scriptures of religions to a certain extent but in reality they cannot lead us all the way as we are to rely on spiritual experience alone; our spiritual experiences becoming our guide.

In Honour of Satguru Kabir

Satguru Kabir ranks among the world's greatest poets. In India, he is perhaps the most quoted author. He lived perhaps during 1398-1518 and is thought to have lived longer than 100 years. He had enormous influence on Indian philosophy and Hindi poetry.

His birth and death are surrounded by legends. He grew up in a Muslim weaver family, but some say he was really son of a Brahmin widow who was adopted by a childless couple. When he died his Hindu and Muslim followers started fighting about the last rites. The legend is that when they lifted the cloth covering his body, they found flowers instead. The Muslim followers buried their half and the Hindu cremated their half. In Maghar, his tomb and samadhi still stand side by side.

Satguru Kabir's writings have greatly influenced mysticism, especially the Bhakti movement. His compositions have a uniquely powerful style, expressing his own spiritual awakening, urging others to wake up and observe the delusions in individuals and society. His poems resonate with praise for the true guru who reveals the divine through direct experience.

"Between the poles of the conscious and the unconscious, there has the mind made a swing.

Thereon hang all beings and all worlds, and that swing never ceases its sway.

Millions of beings are there - the sun and the moon in their courses are there.

Millions of ages pass, and the swing goes on. All swing!

The sky and the earth and the air and the water and the Lord Himself taking form.

And the sight of this has made Kabir a servant."

~ Satguru Kabir

APPENDIX 1 – Overview and 5 Principles of the Conscious Meditation Foundation

The principle of nonviolence - "*ahimsa*" - or loving kindness, as it is best understood in the English language, is the most distinctive and well-known aspect of our spiritual practice, which is in common with Jainism. The understanding and implementation of loving-kindness is more radical, scrupulous, and comprehensive on this path than is common in many spiritual traditions. Non-violence and its active principal of loving-kindness are seen as the most essential and conscious practices for everyone.

A conscientious and thorough application of loving-kindness towards everyday activities, and especially towards food and all living beings, is the most significant hallmark of our spiritual identity. Hence, the diet, is completely **vegetarian**, and usually excludes onions and garlic. Lacto-vegetarianism represents the minimal spiritual practice. Food, which contains even small particles of the bodies of dead animals, is absolutely unacceptable.

The spiritual practice is for all to make considerable efforts in everyday life not to injure nature or plants any more than is necessary in order to live a healthy and balanced life.

The following five vows are conscious intentions that encourage spiritual development and deepen ones **meditation** through the cultivation of personal wisdom through deep awareness. There are different levels of vows or conscious intentions for monastic practitioners and worldly practitioners of a spiritual lifestyle. Both undertake the five major vows as the core active principal of spiritual practice and worldly everyday living.

1.: Nonviolence

Non-Violence, or '**Ahimsa,**' means loving-kindness and is a term meaning 'not to injure'. The word is derived from the Sanskrit root *hiṃs* – to strike; *hiṃsā* is injury or harm, *a-hiṃsā* is the opposite of this, i.e. cause no injury, do no harm. Ahimsa is a multidimensional concept, inspired by the premise that all living beings share the spark of the divine spiritual energy; to hurt another being is to hurt oneself. Ahimsa is also related to the notion that any violence has karmic consequences. This principle of Ahimsa or loving-kindness is the concept and primary principal, which our ethical philosophy and **meditation** practice has as its basis. Ahimsa's precept of 'cause no injury' includes causing no injury by one's deeds, words, and thoughts.

2.: Truth and Sincerity

'Satya' is a Sanskrit word that loosely translates into English as "unchangeable", "that which pervades the universe in all its constancy". Satya is the principle of integration embedded in Supreme Consciousness and experienced through **meditation**. By being fully aware, alert and conscious of the constantly moving present moment, one naturally experiences their true nature, that which is unchangeable; hence, the very important recommendation of maintaining a daily practice of meditation, as an integral aspect of ones lifestyle.

Satya is also interpreted as "absolute truth" or "reality". Figuratively it means truth. This vow is to always speak and base all ones actions from truth. Given that non-violence has priority, other principles yield to it whenever they conflict: in a situation where speaking truth could lead to violence, silence is to be observed.

3.: Total Honesty in all Behaviours

'Asteya' means to not take anything that is not willingly offered. Attempting to extort material wealth or gain from others or to exploit the weak comes from selfish needs and desires that create the belief that who you are is limited to those selfish belief systems and actions rather than to the honouring of the abundance and completeness beyond such limitations. This vow demands total honesty in behaviour and is not just limited to money and wealth.

4.: Chastity

The vow of **'Brahmacharya'** means refraining from all indulgences lacking the essential quality of love and consciousness, including sexual activity, and can also be known as chastity.

The word *brahmacharya* stems literally from two components:

Brahma, (shortened from brahman), the absolute, eternal, supreme and *charya*, which means "to follow". This is often translated as activity, mode of behaviour, or a "virtuous" way of life.

Thus, the word *brahmacharya* indicates a lifestyle adopted to enable one to attain the ultimate reality.

Brahmacharya can also be interpreted more generally in a variety of ways, such as:

- Pursuing 'virtue' however defined. *Brahmacharya* understood in this sense is similar to the classical Greek concept of excellence.

- Clearing underlying personality conflicts, and centering oneself and ones spiritual journey in clear, well conceived and sustainable values.

- Refining one's 'energies' (prana/chi/aura etc.) in relation to other people generally, to become aware of more subtle energies and to take one's energies or 'vibration' to a higher level of consciousness.

5.: Non-Attachment

'Aparigraha' is the concept of non-possessiveness or non-greediness. The term usually means to limit possessions to what is necessary or important, which changes with the time period and depends on need rather than greed. *Aparigraha* is the Sanksrit word for greedlessness or non-grasping. It comes from the word *parigraha*, which means reaching out for something and claiming it for oneself; by adding the 'A' it becomes the antonym. *Aparigraha*, unlike *Asteya*, means taking what is truly necessary and no more. The spiritual dilemma is that people form attachments to possessions. They hoard their wealth and desire more possessions: possessions become an end unto themselves rather than a conscious presence to what is beyond such attachments.

The below points help clarify how to put this vow into practice.

- It is good karma to use surplus possessions to benefit others.

- It is good karma to live simply.
- An ideal is to live on half of ones income, save a quarter of ones income for old age, or for times of sickness, and give the last quarter to charity or a spiritual cause.

Very few modern worldly practitioners are able to follow, to the letter, the vows given above, and in fact it would be very difficult to do so, but with ones heartfelt intention to follow the spirit of the vows, being the fundamental key to start to know the self, then naturally and without effort we are able to follow these vows. Without wisdom and knowing the self, following the vows becomes simply an external practice.

Spirituality is the gradual process to awakening through self-awareness, selfless service and meditation. To the extent that the ego is attuned to the divine, to that extent, divinity manifests in one's life. Through the means of meditation the mind acquires new ways of knowing the deeper levels of reality, culminating in the mind-transcending realization of pure Consciousness. Meaning that, through ones clear understanding of wisdom and the above 5 Principles it is possible to be "free" here and now.

APPENDIX 2 – Resources

The Path of the Heart

With the guidance of Sat Tony Samara, discover a path of profound transformation, evolution of consciousness and inner peace. This path is open to all people from all walks of life, who seek Health, Happiness and Inner Wisdom - http://www.TonySamara.com.

Conscious Meditation Energy Transmissions

Online courses are open to everyone. The only requirement is that participants are willing to open themselves to the knowledge that is universal and present in each and all, and by its very essence creates one's unique spiritual path. http://www.tonysamara.co.uk/blog/satsangs/.

Tony Samara Books

Books of timeless inspiration and practical wisdom!

"The outside world doesn't form our state of consciousness - rather it challenges us to make a choice. A choice where we hear the voice of truth as it gently invites us away from the madness that we have created for ourselves. A choice, that invites us to transcend the world of the unconscious, by remaining fully absorbed in the present moment." - Sat Tony Samara.
http://www.tonysamarabooks.com.

Our Beautiful World

We live in such a beautiful world. We invite you to visit the links we recommend on the pages of this website in order to realise just how lucky we are to be alive on the planet at this time, and realise the freedom that you have for making a conscious choice that will make a difference - http://www.OurBeautifulWorld.org.

You can also find Tony Samara inspiring videos on YouTube:
http://www.youtube.com/samarafoundation.

APPENDIX 3 - Frequently Asked Questions

Q: I would like to be able to listen to Tony Samara's online satsangs. How is this possible?

A: Tony Samara conducts many online satsangs in various formats. There are daily satsangs for those who are interested in joining the residents of the Garden of Light in their morning satsangs Monday to Friday and energy transmission satsangs of a longer duration on Sundays. There are also special event satsangs from time to time. These events are all possible to locate at http://www.tonysamara.co.uk/blog/satsangs/.

Q: I would like to support the Conscious Meditation Foundation. How can I do this?

A: Thank you for your question. Here is a list of 13 ways to support the CMF:

• Meditate DAILY for 15 minutes or more using the Third Eye Meditation (http://www.thethirdeyemeditation.com) or choose any other of Tony Samara's meditations.

• Utilise the Mantra "Hu Satya Naam" or the Namokar Mantra to address situations of stress and conflict (inwardly and outwardly).

• Create a Conscious Meditation Group in your area. Get together and Meditate with like-minded people using Tony Samara's Satsangs and Meditations. Connection is the key!

• Select books and ebooks for yourself, or as gifts for family and friends, from http://www.TonySamaraBooks.com.

• Order copies of Tony Samara's NEW AudioBook http://goo.gl/vcB3HO.

• Watch and listen FREE to Tony Samara's Meditational and Inspirational videos from YouTube http://www.youtube.com/samarafoundation. Gather your friends and watch/listen to them together.

• Make a direct donation to CMF to support the various projects and assist in offsetting administrative and production costs http://www.tonysamara.com/english/donate/. You may also like to consider a recurrent donation or leave a legacy in your last will and testament to provide support for future generations.

• Implement a vegetarian diet — the physical body is our temple and eating a vegetarian diet rich in products that are organic and full of life force is encouraged.

• Join Tony Samara for Satsang. For more information http://www.tonysamara.co.uk/blog/satsangs.

• Become an active participant in Tony Samara's Blog http://www.tonysamara.co.uk/blog.

• Hold a Fundraising event — Raise funds while doing something you enjoy, in your own city, in a different country, choosing the theme that compels you most and is close to your heart.

• Calling for Global Talent from around the world. We would love to hear from people who can assist our online efforts to share the CMF's message around the world. We especially seek translators in any language, English language transcribers and people with literacy skills in any language.

• Share this information with your friends.

NB. The Conscious Meditation Foundation is a non-profit organisation. All money made from the sale of books, booklets, CD's, and all other products, goes directly back into the work of the CMF.

Thank you for your help in bringing this vision into reality.

TONY SAMARA

www.TonySamaraBooks.com
info@tonysamara.org

Through the use of this healing symbol and by keeping this book close at hand you are creating an Intentional Space of Peace. The transference of 'Universal Energy,' through the book, may allow for gentle self-healing to happen and the creation of a state of equilibrium that brings the beautiful qualities of Joy, Happiness and Well-being into your life and the life of your loved ones.

Lightning Source UK Ltd.
Milton Keynes UK
UKOW07f0642080415

249289UK00012B/37/P